AI WORLD
AI IN ENTERTAINMENT

by Ford Chambers

Ideas for Parents and Teachers

Pogo Books let children practice reading informational text while introducing them to nonfiction features such as headings, labels, sidebars, maps, and diagrams, as well as a table of contents, glossary, and index.

Carefully leveled text with a strong photo match offers early fluent readers the support they need to succeed.

Before Reading

- "Walk" through the book and point out the various nonfiction features. Ask the student what purpose each feature serves.
- Look at the glossary together. Read and discuss the words.

Read the Book

- Have the child read the book independently.
- Invite them to list questions that arise from reading.

After Reading

- Discuss the child's questions. Talk about how they might find answers to those questions.
- Prompt the child to think more. Ask: Would you like to watch a show made entirely by AI? Why or why not?

Pogo Books are published by Jump!
5357 Penn Avenue South
Minneapolis, MN 55419
www.jumplibrary.com

Copyright © 2025 Jump! International copyright reserved in all countries. No part of this book may be reproduced in any form without written permission from the publisher.

Library of Congress Cataloging-in-Publication Data is available at www.loc.gov or upon request from the publisher.

ISBN: 979-8-89213-562-7 (hardcover)
ISBN: 979-8-89213-563-4 (paperback)
ISBN: 979-8-89213-564-1 (ebook)

Editor: Alyssa Sorenson
Designer: Emma Almgren-Bersie

Photo Credits: Shutterstock, cover; PeopleImages - Yuri A/Shutterstock, 1; Prostock-Studio/iStock, 3; Master1305/Shutterstock, 4; Muhammad Ishaq/Dreamstime, 5 (screen); Shutterstock, 5 (hands); SuPatMaN/Shutterstock, 6-7; SeventyFour/Shutterstock, 8; LightField Studios/Shutterstock, 9; Gorodenkoff/Shutterstock, 10-11; SeventyFour Images/Alamy, 12-13; South_agency/iStock, 14-15; Shutterstock, 16-17; kitith/Dreamstime, 18 (screen); JACKREZNOR/Shutterstock, 18 (TV); StockImageFactory/Shutterstock, 19; Rawpixel/Shutterstock, 20-21; iLexx/iStock, 23 (robot); Zuhria Alfitra/iStock, 23 (screen).

Printed in the United States of America at Corporate Graphics in North Mankato, Minnesota.

TABLE OF CONTENTS

CHAPTER 1
What Is AI?....................................4

CHAPTER 2
AI on the Screen............................8

CHAPTER 3
Watching the Future.....................18

ACTIVITIES & TOOLS
Try This!.......................................22
Glossary......................................23
Index...24
To Learn More.............................24

CHAPTER 1
WHAT IS AI?

You watch a show on your tablet. The last **episode** ends. But you want to watch more. An **app** asks for ideas. You type them in. The app **generates** a new episode just for you!

How does it do this? It uses **artificial intelligence** (AI). AI lets computers do things humans use knowledge and skills to do.

People who work in **entertainment** use AI. This includes people who work on movies, shows, and music. How does AI help them? It writes stories. It creates pictures and videos. It works with sounds, too. AI is changing entertainment!

> **DID YOU KNOW?**
>
> Why do people work with AI? It is fast. People can make more movies, shows, and music. It saves companies money, too.

CHAPTER 1

CHAPTER 2

AI ON THE SCREEN

Moviemakers use AI. How? Each movie needs a **script**. Writers make one. AI reads it. Then AI suggests ways to make it better.

script

Who would be the best actor for a movie? Where is the best place to shoot a scene? AI could suggest these, too.

CHAPTER 2

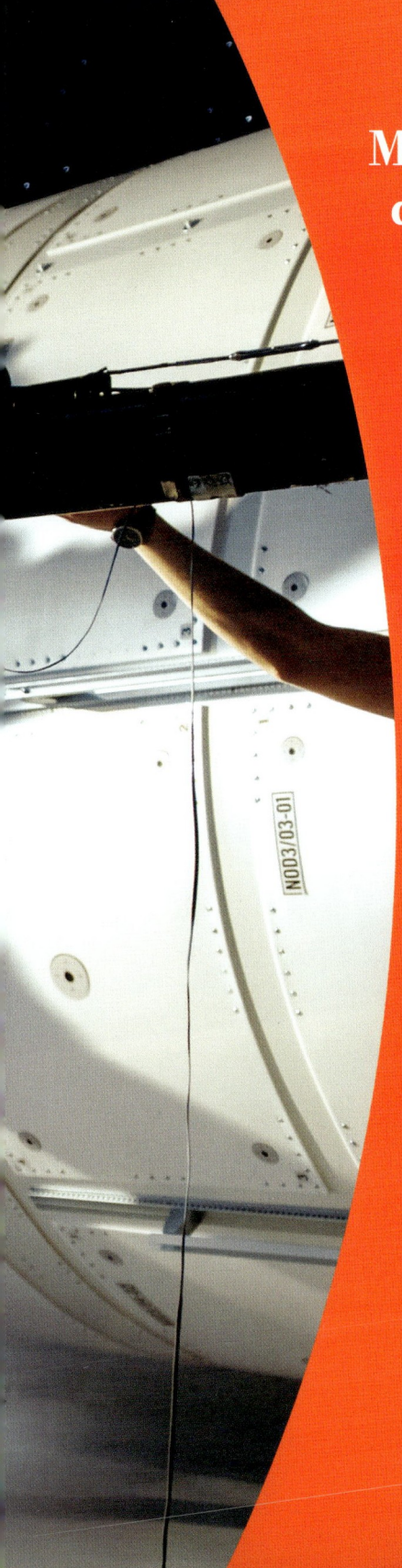

Movies may have **animations** and **special effects**. These take a long time for people to make. But AI creates them quickly. AI frees up people's time for other work.

AI can change the look on an actor's face. It can erase objects, too. Maybe ropes held up an actor. AI makes it look like the actor flies through the air!

DID YOU KNOW?

AI can give an actor a new face. The actor can look younger. Or the actor can look like a completely different person!

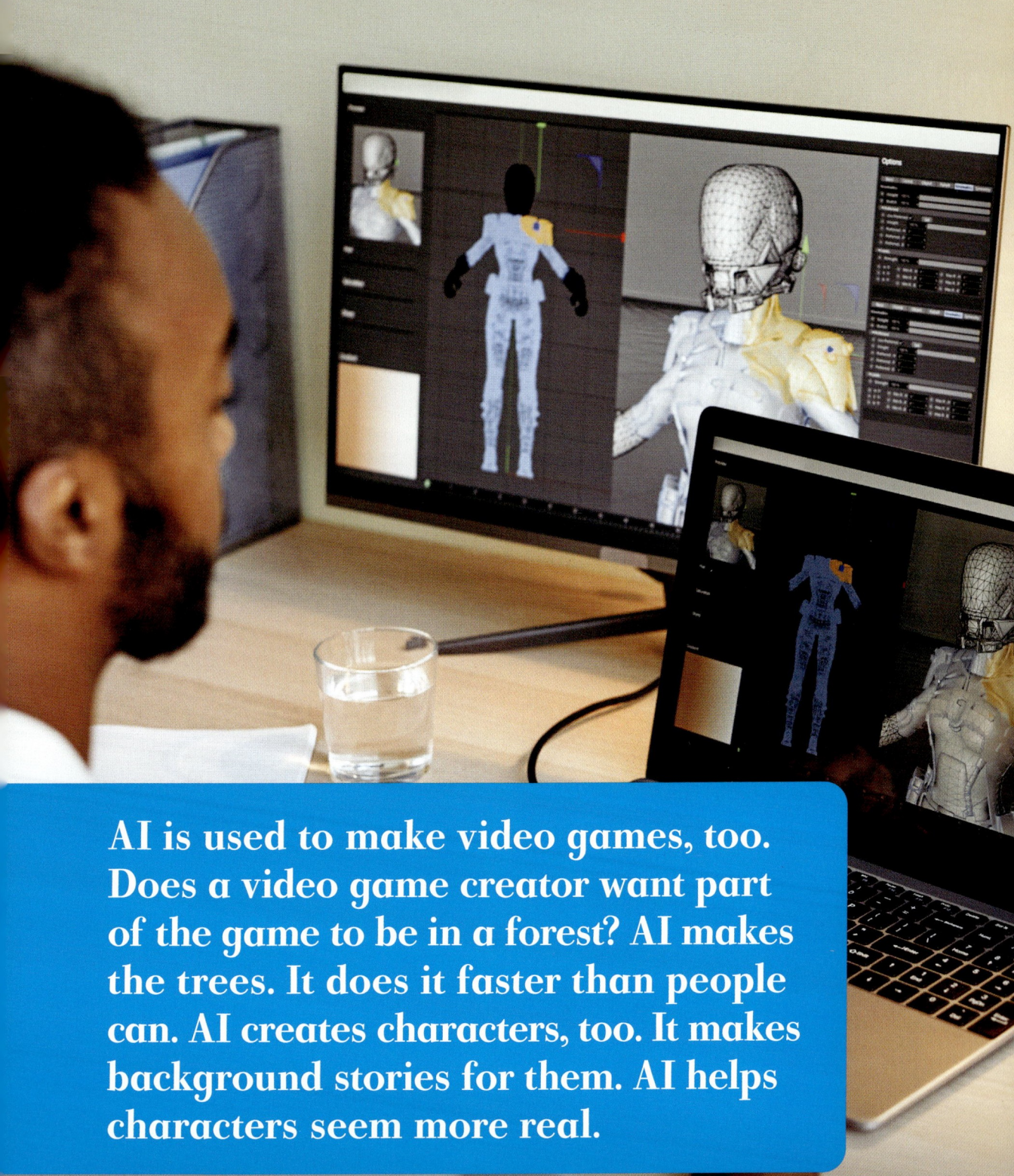

AI is used to make video games, too. Does a video game creator want part of the game to be in a forest? AI makes the trees. It does it faster than people can. AI creates characters, too. It makes background stories for them. AI helps characters seem more real.

TAKE A LOOK!

What percentage of video game creators used AI in 2024? Take a look!

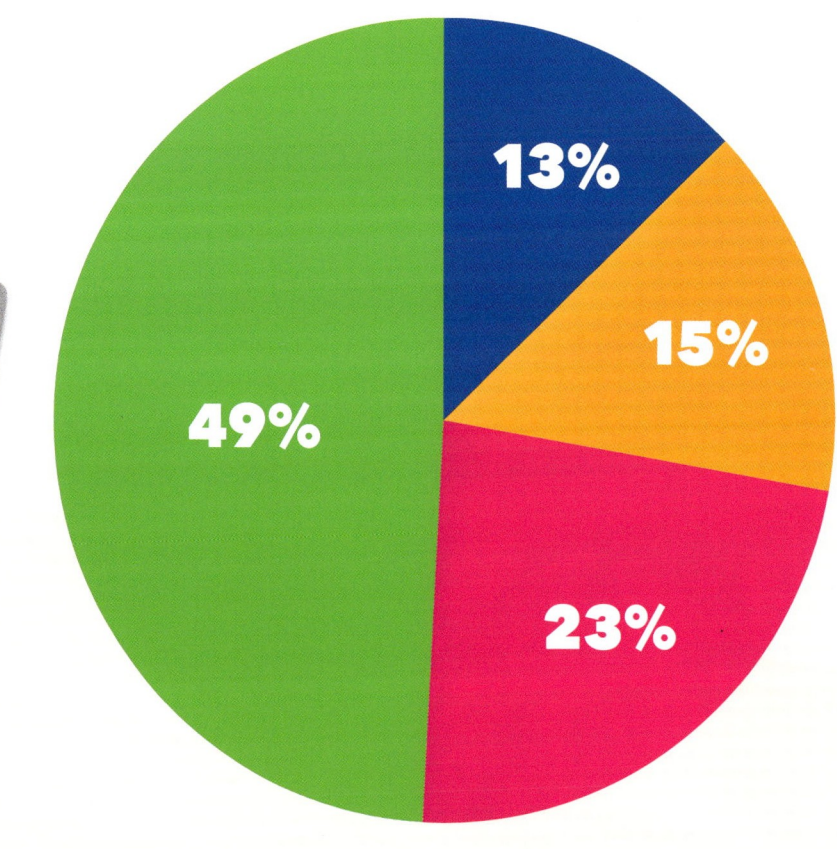

- Already using AI
- Do not want to use AI
- Interested in using AI in the future
- Other

Musicians use AI, too. Did a pianist hit the wrong key? That is OK! AI fixes the sound. It can also delete background noise from a recording.

AI creates music. It can copy a musician's voice. It learns their style. It makes new songs in that style.

DID YOU KNOW?

AI can write songs. People tell AI what they want a song to be about. AI writes the lyrics!

CHAPTER 2

There is so much to watch and listen to. AI learns what we like. It suggests new shows and songs. Do you watch a lot of sports? Maybe you also like history shows. AI might suggest a movie about a sports team in the 1930s!

CHAPTER 2

CHAPTER 3
WATCHING THE FUTURE

Someday, AI could do more for movies and shows. AI could make many things on a computer! Towns, castles, and roads could all be special effects. People wouldn't have to spend time and money building **sets**.

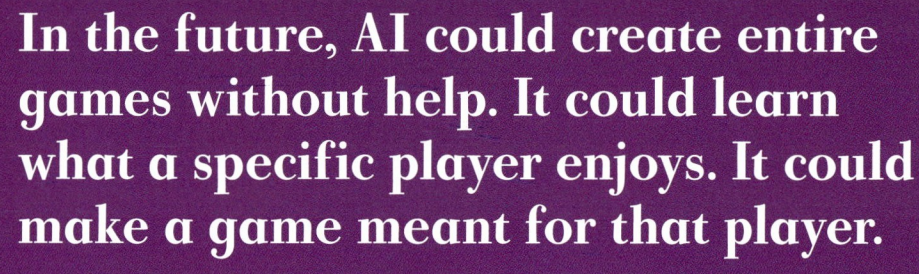

In the future, AI could create entire games without help. It could learn what a specific player enjoys. It could make a game meant for that player.

Movies and shows might get more **interactive**. Viewers could ask AI to make a new ending for a movie. Or they could tell AI to put them into the story. Someday, you could be on the screen!

ACTIVITIES & TOOLS

> **TRY THIS!**

MAKE A MOVIE WITH AI

What sort of movie could AI help you create? Come up with ideas with this fun activity!

What You Need:
- paper and pencil or a device for taking notes

1. Think of a movie idea. Where will your movie take place? Who are the characters? What will happen in the story?
2. Write out a few scenes. Detail what happens.
3. Make a list of what your movie needs. This could include sets, costumes, makeup, and special effects.
4. Think of ways for AI to help. Write down your ideas. Share them with a friend or family member.

GLOSSARY

animations: Moving images created from pictures or drawings.

app: A computer program.

artificial intelligence: The science of making computers do things that previously needed human intelligence, such as understanding language.

entertainment: The business of creating shows, movies, music, and other things for people to enjoy.

episode: One of the programs in a show.

generates: Creates or produces something.

interactive: Letting users make choices that change parts of a game or show.

script: The written story of a movie or show.

sets: Sceneries for movies or shows.

special effects: Illusions made by computers for use in movies or shows.

INDEX

actor 9, 11
animations 11
app 4
characters 12
computers 5, 18
episode 4
erase 11
generates 4
ideas 4
interactive 21
lyrics 15
money 6, 18

moviemakers 8
musicians 15
recording 15
scene 9
script 8
sets 18
songs 15, 16
sounds 6, 15
special effects 11, 18
suggests 8, 9, 16
video games 12, 13, 19
writes 6, 15

TO LEARN MORE

Finding more information is as easy as 1, 2, 3.

① Go to www.factsurfer.com
② Enter "Alinentertainment" into the search box.
③ Choose your book to see a list of websites.